かわいいパン

Kawaii
Bread

LITTLE MISS BENTO
SHIRLEY WONG

Marshall Cavendish
Cuisine

The publisher wishes to thank Lovera Collections for the loan of the tableware used in this publication.

Editor: Lydia Leong
Designer: Benson Tan
Photographer: Calvin Tan

Published by Marshall Cavendish Cuisine
An imprint of Marshall Cavendish International

A member of the
Times Publishing Group

Other Marshall Cavendish Offices:
Marshall Cavendish Corporation. 99 White Plains Road, Tarrytown NY 10591-9001, USA • Marshall Cavendish International (Thailand) Co Ltd. 253 Asoke, 12th Flr, Sukhumvit 21 Road, Klongtoey Nua, Wattana, Bangkok 10110, Thailand • Marshall Cavendish (Malaysia) Sdn Bhd, Times Subang, Lot 46, Subang Hi-Tech Industrial Park, Batu Tiga, 40000 Shah Alam, Selangor Darul Ehsan, Malaysia

National Library Board, Singapore Cataloguing-in-Publication Data

Name(s): Wong, Shirley (Writer on bento cooking) | Tan, Calvin, photographer.
Title: Kawaii bread / Little Miss Bento, Shirley Wong ; photographer, Calvin Tan.
Description: Singapore : Marshall Cavendish Cuisine, [2017]
Identifier(s): OCN 979999733 | ISBN 978-981-47-7173-3 (paperback)
Subject(s): LCSH: Bread. | Baking.
Classification: DDC 641.815--dc23

Printed by Times Offset (M) Sdn Bhd

This book is for my nephew, the little ray of sunshine
who has brought so much joy to my family.

Acknowledgements

As I am writing this, my heart is filled with much warmth and appreciation for all the support I have received, from my family, my better half and friends.

To those who have requested to have my kawaii bread recipes, this book is my way of showing my gratitude for your support. Please enjoy making these cute breads.

Working on this project has not been easy, but I am thankful to have had the opportunity to do this. I would like to thank my editor, Lydia Leong, designer, Benson Tan, and photographer, Calvin Tan, for their partnership in putting together this beautiful cookbook.

Contents

Introduction

I am a lover of all things kawaii and delicious, and this is exactly what you will enjoy in this cookbook.

Within these pages, I have included my favourite kawaii bread recipes with step-by-step photographs, baking tips and ideas for all who love not just baking bread, but making them kawaii!

May you have fun using the recipes in this book to make bread to enjoy with your family and friends!

Shirley Wong
Little Miss Bento

Basic Tools & Equipment

The tools and equipment for decorative bread-making are available from baking supply stores and supermarkets. The following pages highlight the basic tools and equipment I find most useful.

Baking Paper

Line baking trays with baking paper to make it easier to remove the buns from the trays after baking.

Cling Wrap

When leaving bread dough to rest, cover it with cling wrap to reduce moisture loss.

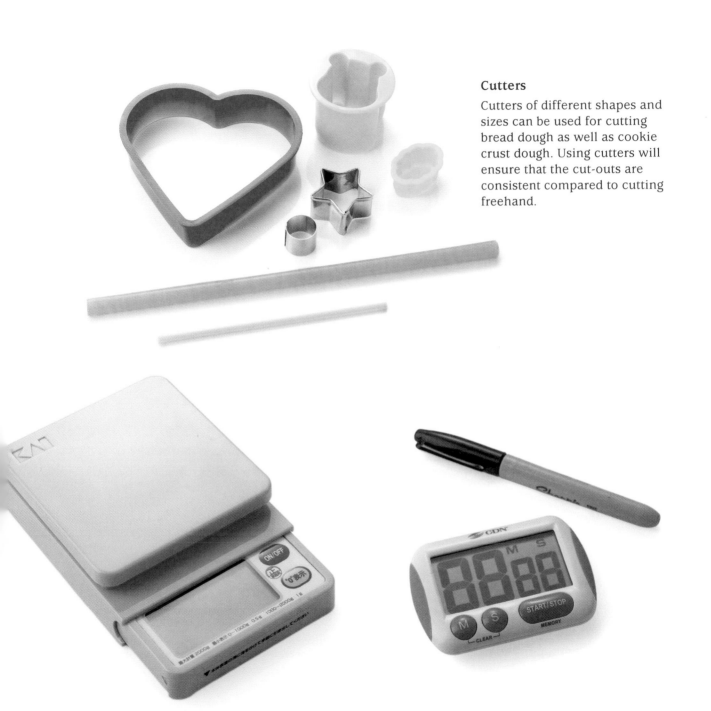

Cutters

Cutters of different shapes and sizes can be used for cutting bread dough as well as cookie crust dough. Using cutters will ensure that the cut-outs are consistent compared to cutting freehand.

Digital Kitchen Weighing Scale

In making character designs and pull-apart breads, it is helpful to be able to divide the dough evenly to ensure that the final design looks balanced. Precise measurements with the help of a digital scale will aid in this process.

Digital Timer and Marker

It is important to time the fermentation process to avoid over-fermenting the bread dough. A digital timer will help keep time. Marking the time on the cling wrap will also help you to keep tabs.

Measuring Cups and Spoons

For the recipes in this book, a 250-ml measuring cup and a regular set of measuring spoons (1 Tbsp, 1 tsp, $1/2$ tsp and $1/4$ tsp) will suffice for measuring wet and dry ingredients. A 20-ml measuring cup is also handy, but not essential.

Mixing Bowls

Mixing bowls are used to mix the basic bread dough and to let the dough rest.

Pastry Scraper

This simple tool is very useful for bread-making. I use it to transfer the bread dough from the bowl to the worktop, and to cut and divide the dough.

Pastry brush

A soft pastry brush is useful for applying egg wash on dough and for brushing off excess flour.

Rolling Pin

A rolling pin is useful for shaping certain designs of bread. It can also be used to degas the dough.

Scissors

Having a pair of small, sharp scissors on hand is useful when the design of the bread requires trimming or cutting to achieve its shape.

Rolling Pin Guides

Rolling pin guides are not essential, but they help make the work of rolling out cookie crust dough in an even layer much easier.

Wooden Spatula

A spatula with a good grip helps with mixing the ingredients for the dough.

Sieve

A sieve is useful for sifting ingredients such as matcha powder and cocoa powder to remove any lumps, or for dusting icing sugar on the finished product.

Baking Pans and Moulds

A variety of baking pans, cups and moulds can be used to present the breads in an appealing way. I use ring moulds and the funnel from a chiffon cake pan to make pull-apart breads. I also bake bread in cake moulds and pans of different shapes for more variety. Feel free to experiement!

Basic Ingredients

These are some of the common ingredients used in the recipes in this book. Most of the ingredients are available from supermarkets, while some of the more specialised items may be purchased from baking supply stores or online.

DRY INGREDIENTS

Bread Flour

Bread flour has a higher protein content than other types of flour and this helps with the development of gluten which gives bread its chewy and elastic texture.

Castor Sugar

This is a finely granulated sugar that can be more easily incorporated into mixtures given its fine texture.

Instant Dry Yeast

I use instant dry yeast to make bread as it dissolves quickly and activates quickly too. The recipes in this book have been developed based on using instant dry yeast.

Skimmed Milk Powder

Milk powder adds flavour to bread dough and gives the baked bread a softer texture. Some baking supply stores stock milk powder in small quantities.

WET INGREDIENTS

Eggs

Eggs are not a main ingredient in bread dough. I use egg yolks mixed with milk and a little salt to add colour and shine to the surface of buns.

Glucose

Glucose has two key roles in baking bread. It acts as a flavour enhancer and sweetener, and also helps to add moisture and tenderness to baked bread.

Milk

Liquid milk is not a main ingredient in bread dough. I use it to dilute dry colouring agents such as matcha or cocoa powder to make it easier to mix into the dough. For this, water can be used in place of milk.

Unsalted Butter

Butter adds flavour and moisture to bread dough. It helps retain the gases released during baking and helps bread remain soft and fresh for at least a few days. I use unsalted butter to help control the amount of salt added to the dough.

INGREDIENTS FOR COLOURING AND FLAVOURING

Bamboo Charcoal Powder

This is a popular ingredient used in baking and is available from baking supply stores. It is said to have many health benefits, but I use it mainly for the rich dark colour it adds to baking as it is flavourless.

Cocoa Powder

I use cocoa powder for flavour and colour in making bread. If you are able to find black cocoa powder (far left), you can use it in place of bamboo charcoal powder to achieve a dark colour dough with a cocoa flavour.

Dehydrated Vegetable Powders

Vegetable powders are made from real vegetables and fruit. They are a good alternative to artificial food colouring, although the colours will not be as vibrant.

Green Tea Powder

Green tea powder adds a lovely natural green colour and rich flavour to bread. Use good quality matcha powder for the best results.

Instant Coffee Powder

Instant coffee powder adds flavour and colour to bread dough. Use good quality coffee powder for the best flavour. It is also advisable to use fine powder for better results.

Pumpkin Purée

Pumpkin purée adds both colour and taste to bread dough. Although it is available in cans from the supermarket, you can make your own by cooking fresh pumpkin in the microwave oven, or by steaming or boiling. Once tender, peel the skin and mash.

INGREDIENTS FOR DECORATION AND ASSEMBLY

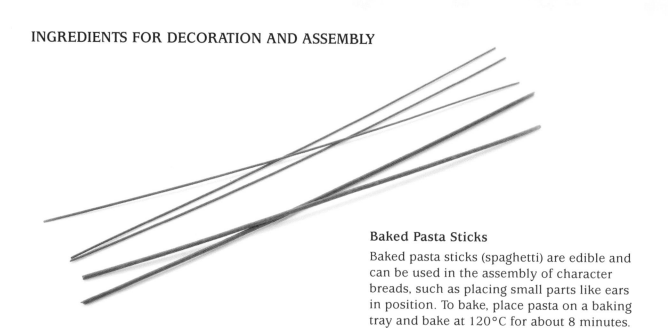

Baked Pasta Sticks

Baked pasta sticks (spaghetti) are edible and can be used in the assembly of character breads, such as placing small parts like ears in position. To bake, place pasta on a baking tray and bake at 120°C for about 8 minutes.

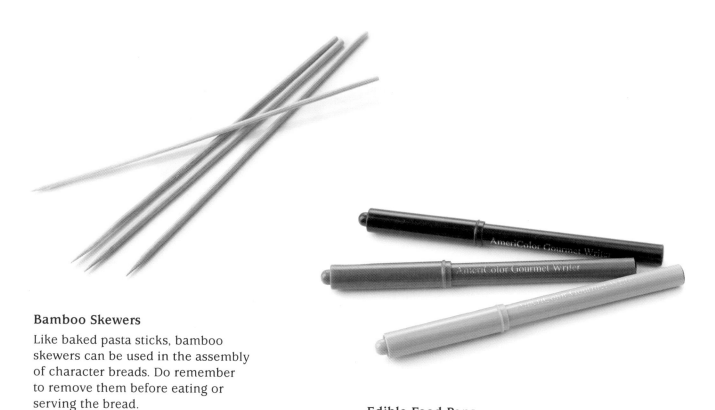

Bamboo Skewers

Like baked pasta sticks, bamboo skewers can be used in the assembly of character breads. Do remember to remove them before eating or serving the bread.

Edible Food Pens

These come in a wide range of colours and are a convenient way of adding colour and detail to baked character bread.

Melted Chocolate and Chocolate Pens

I use melted chocolate to attach small parts, such as ears and limbs, to character breads. I also use it to draw features on bread. Store-bought chocolate pens come in a wide range of colours and are a convenient way to draw features on bread.

Royal Icing

Royal icing is used to decorate cookies and cakes. I use it to draw features on character breads. To prepare, combine 200 g icing sugar, 5 g meringue powder and 2 Tbsp water in a bowl and mix well with a whisk until mixture is firm. Add a little food colouring if desired. Spoon into a small piping bag and make a small cut at the tip for piping.

Sprinkles

These edible decorations are made of sugar. They come in a variety of shapes and colours. Be creative in using sprinkles to add colour to your character breads.

Basic Techniques

MAKING BASIC BREAD DOUGH

Ingredients			Baker's Percentage
Bread flour	160 g	200 g	100%
Skimmed milk powder	2 tsp	2¹/₂ tsp	3.75%
Castor sugar	1 Tbsp	1¹/₄ Tbsp	7.5%
Glucose	10 g	12.5 g	6.25%
Instant dry yeast	1 tsp	1¹/₄ tsp	1.9%
Water	90 ml	112.5 ml	56.3%
Salt	¹/₂ tsp	²/₃ tsp	0.9%
Unsalted butter	20 g	25 g	12.5%
Additional dry ingredients (such as cocoa or matcha powder) for single coloured dough. For multicoloured dough, see page 24.	About 1 tsp	About 1¹/₄ tsp or adjust as required	2%

NOTE The table above lists the proportion of ingredients needed for the recipes in this book. You can scale the quantities as required based on the baker's percentage provided.

22

1. Measure all the ingredients and have them ready. In a bowl, add sugar, glucose, instant dry yeast and 20 ml water. Mix well with a spatula.

2. Add half the bread flour and all the skimmed milk powder. Mix well.

3. Add the remaining water and mix vigorously. There may be some air pockets/bubbles. This is a good sign that the yeast has been activated.

4. Add the remaining bread flour, salt and butter. Mix until it all comes together in a rough mixture.

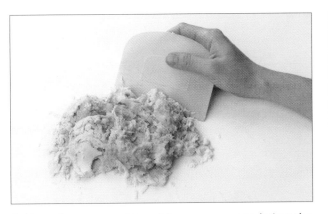

5. Transfer to a worktop. Use a scraper to bring the dough together, then knead for about 10 minutes until the dough is smooth. When kneading, use one hand to hold the dough and the other hand to stretch out the dough.

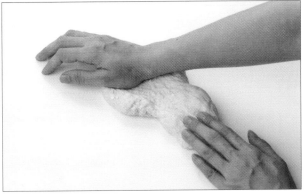

6. Repeat to roll the dough, rotate its position and roll again. If the dough is too sticky, pick it up and slam it down on the worktop. Repeat until the dough is less sticky and you are able to knead it by hand.

COLOURING BREAD DOUGH

This section details how to colour bread dough. If not colouring the dough, skip to step 7 (page 25).

C1. Weigh and divide the dough into the required portions.

C2. If using dry ingredients, add a little milk/water to create a paste. This will make it easier to mix.

C3. Add the colouring to the dough and knead until the dough is smooth and reaches the window pane stage. See step 8 (page 25).

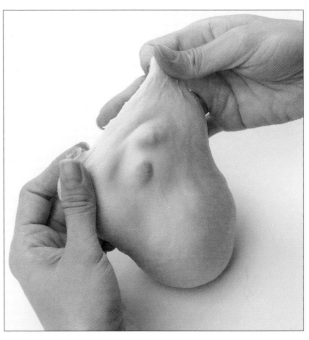

7. The dough will gain elasticity as the gluten forms. It will also look smoother. Relax the dough by continually cupping it in your hands in a sort of V-shape until it is smooth and reaches the window pane stage.

8. At the window pane stage, the dough will be smooth and elastic. It will not stick to your hands. To test, stretch the dough gently until you are able to see your fingers through it. The dough will look smooth and will not tear easily.

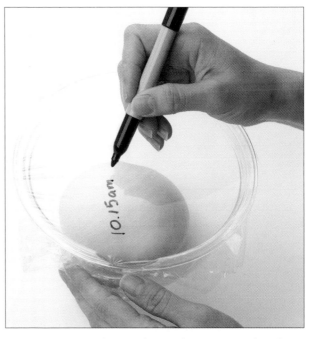

9. Shape the dough into a rough ball and place in a mixing bowl. Cover the bowl with cling wrap.

10. You may wish to indicate the time on the cling wrap to avoid over-fermenting the dough.

FIRST FERMENTATION

11. Leave the dough to ferment at room temperature for 50–60 minutes. During this time, the dough will increase 1.5 to 2 times in size. Do not disturb the dough as it will affect the fermentation process. Some ovens have a fermentation function and the process may take 25–30 minutes.

12. To check the fermentation, dust a finger with some bread flour, stick it into the dough up to the knuckle, then pull it out. If the indentation remains, the first fermentation is complete. If not, the dough needs more time. Let the dough rest for another 5–10 minutes before checking again.

13. Degas the bread dough by gently and quickly punching it with your fist. Reshape into a ball.

14. Weigh and portion the dough as required in the recipe, then reshape quickly and gently into balls.

15. Cover with cling wrap and let the dough rest for 10 minutes. This is known as bench time. It allows the gluten in the dough to relax and makes it easier to handle, fill and shape.

16. To add a filling to the dough, see page 30. After filling and/or reshaping the dough, assemble the pieces on a lined baking tray or pan as required.

17. You can spray the dough lightly with water to keep the surface moist, then cover it with cling wrap for the final fermentation.

FINAL FERMENTATION AND BAKING

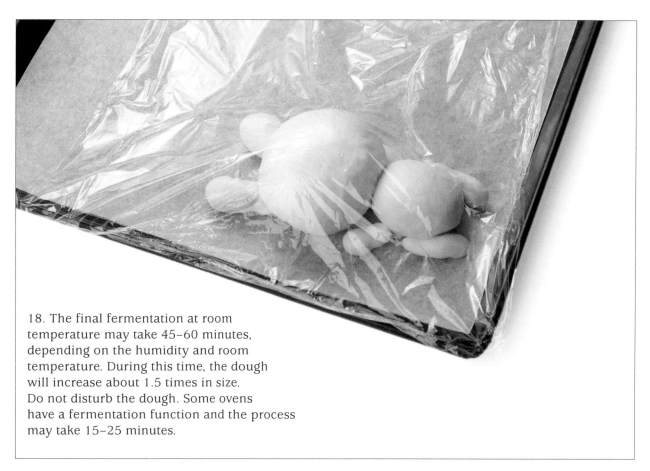

18. The final fermentation at room temperature may take 45–60 minutes, depending on the humidity and room temperature. During this time, the dough will increase about 1.5 times in size. Do not disturb the dough. Some ovens have a fermentation function and the process may take 15–25 minutes.

19. Check the final fermentation by gently pressing the dough with a finger. The dough should bounce back. If not, the dough needs more time.

20. When the dough is ready for baking, you may brush it with egg wash or dust it with flour as required before baking.

21. The baking temperature in these recipes is lower with a longer baking time compared to regular bread. This is to prevent overbrowning while ensuring that the bread is sufficiently baked.

22. Let the bread cool, then decorate as desired.

STUFFING BREAD DOUGH WITH FILLING

Many of the character breads can be enjoyed plain or they can be served with butter, jam and other spreads. You can also stuff them with your favourite filling or with the filling suggested in the recipe. This section details how to stuff the dough with filling after step 16 (page 27).

F1. Weigh and portion out the dough and filling.

F2. Place the dough sealed side facing up.

F3. Flatten the dough using your fingers. Taper it such that the centre of the dough is thicker and the edges thinner.

F4. Place the filling in the centre.

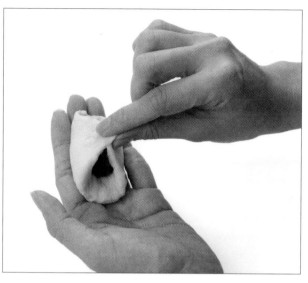

F5. Bring two opposite sides of the dough together to enclose the filling.

F6. Bring another two opposite sides of the dough together to completely enclose the filling.

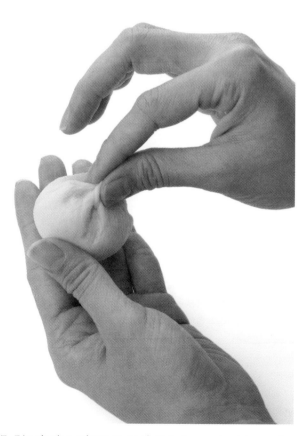

F7. Pinch the edges to seal. It is important to seal the dough well to prevent the filling from flowing out during the baking process.

F8. Place the filled dough sealed side down. Continue with step 17 (page 27) to prepare the dough for final fermentation.

TYPES OF FILLING

Character breads can be filled with almost any type of filling. Here are recipes for some of my favourite home-made fillings. Adjust the ingredients to taste as preferred. Besides making your own fillings, you can also use store-bought fillings such as chocolate, pineapple jam and red bean paste.

CURRY CHICKEN

Ingredients

Sesame oil, as needed

$^1/_4$ medium onion, peeled and diced

$^1/_2$ medium-large potato, peeled and diced

400 ml water

100 g chicken, diced

2 shiitake mushrooms, diced

34 g Japanese curry cube

21 g butter

21 g plain flour

Method

1. In a deep non-stick pan, heat some sesame oil. Fry onion, then potato until onion is cooked and lightly brown. Add about 200 ml water and simmer.

2. In another pan, heat some sesame oil and fry chicken and mushrooms until cooked through. Add to potato mixture and simmer for about 8 minutes.

3. Add curry cube and mix until incorporated. Add remaining water to adjust consistency. The curry should be thick, but not gooey. Continue to simmer for 5 minutes.

4. In the meantime, reheat pan from step 2. Melt butter. Add flour and stir quickly, then add to curry mixture. Cook, stirring until curry is thick and gooey.

5. Let cool before using.

PUMPKIN PURÉE

Ingredients

150 g pumpkin

40 g finely ground almonds

1 Tbsp soft brown sugar

10 g butter

20 g walnuts, toasted and diced

Vegetable oil, as needed

Method

1. Boil or steam the pumpkin until it is cooked and tender.

2. Scrape the pumpkin flesh from the skin and mash finely. Discard the skin.

3. Transfer the mashed pumpkin to a bowl and add ground almonds, sugar, butter and toasted walnuts. Mix well.

4. Use as needed.

CUSTARD CREAM

Ingredients

1 egg yolk

30 g castor sugar

10 g cornflour

100 ml milk

$^1/_2$ tsp vanilla essence or bean paste

Method

1. Using an electric mixer, beat egg yolk and sugar in a heatproof mixing bowl until pale and thick.

2. Add cornflour and mix well. Set aside.

3. Heat milk and vanilla in a small saucepan until mixture comes to a boil.

4. Pour milk mixture into egg mixture while whisking quickly. Return mixture to saucepan and cook over low heat, stirring until custard thickens.

5. Transfer custard to an airtight container and chill for at least 1 hour before using.

BLACK SESAME

Ingredients

30 g unsalted butter

20 g castor sugar

10 g icing sugar

20 g beaten egg

25 g finely ground almonds

35 g finely ground black sesame seeds

Method

1. Using an electric mixer, beat butter and sugar in a mixing bowl until pale.

2. Add icing sugar and mix well.

3. Add egg in 2–3 parts and mix well.

4. Add ground almonds and ground sesame seeds. Mix well.

5. Transfer to an airtight container and chill before using.

MAKING COOKIE CRUST DOUGH

A layer of sweet cookie crust on soft fluffy bread adds an interesting contrast of textures. This cookie crust is also referred to as melon *pan* in Japan. It can be used to create fun designs for character breads.

COOKIE CRUST DOUGH

Ingredients

70 g unsalted butter,
   at room temperature

50 g castor sugar +
   more for dusting

3–5 drops vanilla essence

1–2 drops lemon essence, optional

A little food colouring, optional

2 tsp milk

100 g cake flour, sifted

1. Place butter and sugar in a mixing bowl. Mix well with a spatula.

2. Add essences, food colouring, if using, and milk. Mix well.

3. Add cake flour in 2–3 parts. Mix well after each addition.

4. Mix until cookie dough comes together. Cover with cling wrap and chill for 30–45 minutes.

5. Roll cookie dough out evenly between 2 sheets of cling wrap.

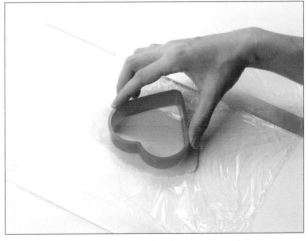

6. Cut out shapes as required. Cover with cling wrap and chill for 30–45 minutes before using.

Frequently Asked Questions

Why did the surface of the bread wrinkle after it was removed from the oven?

There are several reasons for this.

Firstly, the bread may not have been sufficiently baked, due to the differences in the make of different ovens. Try increasing the baking time by 5–8 minutes, then check the base of the bread for colour as this is a good indicator of well-baked bread.

Secondly, the bread could have been over-fermented, leading the dough to expand too much and shrink once it was removed from heat. Monitor the fermentation process closely.

There could also have been too much of a draft when cooling the bread. After removing the bread from the oven, avoid placing it in a location with strong draft.

Why is the texture of the bread gummy after baking?

The most common reason for this is that the bread was under-fermented and the gluten structure was not able to relax. Try increasing the fermentation time and checking that the dough is ready before proceeding with the next step.

Even before the baking time was over, the bread started to brown and the final product wasn't as brightly coloured as it should be. How can this be prevented?

To prevent over browning, place a sheet of aluminium foil or baking paper over the bread during the last 8–10 minutes of baking.

Can I replace bread flour with other types of flour in these recipes?

Bread flour with its high gluten content is the most ideal flour to use in making bread. Gluten is crucial in achieving the springy texture you enjoy in breads.

There are some recipes that call for the addition of cake flour or other low protein flour to complement the bread flour. This helps to soften the texture of the bread, but bread flour remains the key dry ingredient when making bread.

Can these recipes be used with a bread maker?

Yes, you can use a bread maker to knead the dough, if preferred. Follow the instructions that come with your bread maker and note that you may have to increase the quantities in the recipe to meet the minimum quantity required for the bread maker to function.

Baking Tips

Leave room for expansion

When assembling the different parts of a character before leaving it to ferment, always leave some space between each part for the dough to expand. This includes the ears, arms and legs. This will ensure that the parts do not get pushed out of shape when they expand.

Handle different types of fillings

For hard and dry fillings like bean paste or chocolate chips, shape them into balls or chop them up into smaller pieces to help make it easier to wrap them in the dough.

For wet or liquid fillings like custard and spreads, wrap each portion in cling film and refrigerate to set or harden them before using.

Keep parts in place

Use a toothpick or bamboo skewer to connect parts of a character together before baking. This will ensure that the parts stay in place even as the dough expands during baking.

Use baked pasta sticks

Besides using toothpicks and bamboo skewers to connect parts together, you can also use baked pasta sticks (page 20). As these are edible, there is less danger of biting into a toothpick or bamboo skewer should you forget to remove them.

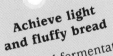

Achieve light and fluffy bread

After the final fermentation is complete, proceed to bake the bread without disturbing or adjusting the dough to ensure that the final baked product is light and fluffy.

Disturbing or adjusting the dough may affect the gluten structure and cause the bread to collapse and harden during baking.

Packaging Ideas

The recipes in this book were designed to produce visually appealing breads that will be perfect as gifts or for bringing along to picnics and parties. Here are some fun wrapping and packaging ideas.

Cute & Cuddly

Plain & Stuffed Buns

Cuddly Cocoa Bear Buns
ココアのくまパン

Makes 6 buns

1 portion basic bread dough using 200 g bread flour (page 22)

5 g cocoa powder, mixed with a little milk/water into a paste

Chocolate chips or chopped chocolate, as needed

White and dark brown/black chocolate pens

1. Prepare basic bread dough (pages 22–25, steps 1–10).

2. Colour dough brown using cocoa powder paste (page 24).

3. Set aside for first fermentation (page 26, steps 11–12).

4. Degas dough and divide into 6 equal portions. Reshape into balls, cover and let rest for 10 minutes (pages 26–27, steps 13–15).

5. Gently punch each portion of dough again to remove gas and further divide each portion to get a head (35 g), a body (17 g), 2 ears (2 g each) and 4 limbs (1.5 g each).

6. Flatten dough for heads and bodies, then stuff with chocolate (pages 30–31). Reshape heads into balls and bodies into ovals. Arrange sealed side down on a lined baking tray.

7. Shape ears into balls and limbs into long ovals and arrange with heads and bodies. Be creative in arranging poses of bears.

8. Set aside for final fermentation (page 28, steps 18–20).

9. Preheat oven to 170°C (top and bottom heat, no fan).

10. Place tray on lowest or second lowest rack in oven and bake for 18–20 minutes.

11. Remove and place on a wire rack to cool.

12. Draw eyes, muzzle and nose with chocolate pens.

13. Tie a ribbon around each bear if desired.

Red Bean Bunny Hop Buns
あずきのうさぎパン

Makes 6 buns

1 portion basic bread dough using 200 g bread flour (page 22)

90 g adzuki bean paste, divided into six 10-g portions and six 5-g portions

Black edible food pen

1. Prepare basic bread dough (pages 22–25, steps 1–10).

2. Set aside for first fermentation (page 26, steps 11–12).

3. Degas dough and divide into 6 equal portions. Reshape into balls, cover and let rest for 10 minutes (pages 26–27, steps 13–15).

4. Gently punch each portion of dough again to remove gas and further divide each portion to get a head (34 g), a body (16 g), 2 ears (3 g each) and 4 limbs (1.5 g each).

5. Flatten dough for heads, then stuff with 10 g bean paste and reshape into balls. Repeat to stuff bodies using remaining bean paste and reshape into ovals (pages 30–31). Arrange sealed side down on a lined baking tray.

6. Shape ears and limbs into long ovals and arrange with heads and bodies. Be creative in arranging poses of bunnies.

7. Set aside for final fermentation (page 28, steps 18–20).

8. Preheat oven to 140°C (top and bottom heat, no fan).

9. Place tray on lowest rack in oven and bake for 20–22 minutes. During final 10–12 minutes of baking, cover buns with a sheet of aluminium foil or baking paper to prevent uneven or over browning.

10. Remove and place on a wire rack to cool.

11. Draw features on bunnies using edible food pen.

Shifty Cats Fun Buns
にゃんこのパン

Makes 7 buns

1 portion basic bread dough using 160 g bread flour (page 22)

Chocolate chips or chopped chocolate, as needed

14 almond slices

3 g adzuki bean paste

Black chocolate pen

Egg Wash

1 egg yolk

2 tsp milk

A pinch of salt

1. Prepare basic bread dough (pages 22–25, steps 1–10).

2. Set aside for first fermentation (page 26, steps 11–12).

3. Degas dough and divide into 7 equal portions. Reshape into balls, cover and let rest for 10 minutes (pages 26–27, steps 13–15).

4. Gently punch each portion of dough again to remove gas and further divide each portion to get a head (25 g), a body (10 g), 2 ears (2 g each) and a tail (2 g).

5. Flatten dough for heads and bodies, then stuff with chocolate and reshape into ovals (pages 30–31). Arrange sealed side down on a lined baking tray.

6. Shape ears into triangles and tails into a longish shape and arrange with heads and bodies. Be creative in arranging tail of cats.

7. Set aside for final fermentation (page 28, steps 18–20).

8. Combine ingredients for egg wash and brush evenly on dough.

9. Place 2 slices of almond on heads for cats' eyes.

10. Shape bean paste into 7 ovals for noses and press one onto each head.

11. Preheat oven to 170°C (top and bottom heat, no fan).

12. Place tray on lowest or second lowest rack in oven and bake for 16–18 minutes.

13. Remove and place on a wire rack to cool.

14. Complete cats' eyes using black chocolate pen.

Woolly Sheep Melon Pan
にゃんこのパン

Makes 6 buns

12 cashews nut halves

1 portion basic bread dough
using 160 g bread flour
(page 22)

1 portion cookie crust dough
(page 34)

Castor sugar, as needed

Black chocolate pen

1. Place cashew nut halves on a lined baking tray and bake at 180°C for 6–8 minutes. Set aside to cool.

2. Prepare basic bread dough (pages 22–25, steps 1–10).

3. Set aside for first fermentation (page 26, steps 11–12).

4. Degas dough and divide into 6 equal portions. Reshape into balls, cover and let rest for 10 minutes (pages 26–27, steps 13–15).

5. Gently punch each portion of dough again to remove gas. Reshape into balls for sheep, taking care to seal edges well (pages 30–31). Place sealed side down on a lined baking tray.

6. Set aside for final fermentation (page 28, steps 18–20).

7. Divide cookie crust dough into 6 equal portions. Roll each portion out on cling film into a circle large enough to cover sheep.

8. Using a knife or a cutter, make a hole in the centre of each cookie crust circle.

9. Using cling film, gently transfer a cookie crust circle onto each ball of dough, shaping cookie crust around dough as necessary.

10. Use a flower cutter to make light indentations on cookie crust to create texture of wool. Dust lightly with sugar.

11. Place 2 cashew nut halves on each sheep for ears.

12. Preheat oven to 160°C (top and bottom heat, no fan).

13. Place tray on lowest rack in oven and bake for 18–20 minutes.

14. Remove and place on a wire rack to cool.

15. Draw features of sheep using black chocolate pen.

Playful Kitten-in-Box Buns
にゃんこのパン

Makes 4 buns

1 portion basic bread dough using 200 g bread flour (page 22)

1 portion curry chicken filling (page 32)

Brown edible food pen

1. Prepare 4 muffin cups for baking bread in. Set aside.

2. Prepare basic bread dough (pages 22–25, steps 1–10).

3. Set aside for first fermentation (page 26, steps 11–12).

4. Degas dough and divide into 4 equal portions. Reshape into balls, cover and let rest for 10 minutes (pages 26–27, steps 13–15).

5. Gently punch each portion of dough again to remove gas and further divide each portion to get a head (60 g), a body (35 g), 2 ears (2 g each) and 2 limbs (1.5 g each) or a tail (4 g).

6. Flatten dough for heads and bodies, then stuff with some curry chicken filling and reshape into balls (pages 30–31).

7. Assemble heads and bodies in muffin cups.

8. Shape ears and limbs or limbs and tail and position on head/body.

9. Set aside for final fermentation (page 28, steps 18–20).

10. Preheat oven to 140°C (top and bottom heat, no fan).

11. Place tray on lowest rack in oven and bake for 20–22 minutes. During final 10–12 minutes of baking, cover buns with a sheet of aluminium foil or baking paper to prevent uneven or over browning.

12. Remove and place on a wire rack to cool.

13. Draw features of kittens using brown edible food pen.

Pop-up Teddy Buns
テディパンのコーン

Makes 5 buns

1 portion basic bread dough
using 200 g bread flour
(page 22)

5 g instant coffee powder
or cocoa powder, mixed
with a little milk/water
into a paste

Baked pasta sticks (page 20)

1 portion royal icing (page 21)

A little black food colouring

1. Prepare 5 ovenproof mugs, each about 7 cm in diameter and 4 cm deep. Set aside.

2. Prepare basic bread dough (pages 22–25, steps 1–10).

3. Colour dough brown using coffee powder or cocoa powder paste (page 24).

4. Set aside for first fermentation (page 26, steps 11–12).

5. Degas dough and divide into 5 equal portions. Reshape into balls, cover and let rest for 10 minutes (pages 26–27, steps 13–15).

6. Gently punch each portion of dough again to remove gas and further divide each portion to get 2 ears (2 g each) and a head.

7. Shape heads round, taking care to seal edges well. Place each head sealed side down in a mug.

8. Shape ears into balls and place on a lined baking tray.

9. Set aside for final fermentation (page 28, steps 18–20).

10. Preheat oven to 160°C (top and bottom heat, no fan).

11. Place tray on lowest or second lowest rack in the oven and bake for 18–20 minutes. Remove ears after 7–8 minutes.

12. Place on a wire rack to cool.

13. Attach ears to heads using baked pasta sticks.

14. Colour half the royal icing black. Spoon black and white royal icing into separate piping bags. Make a small hole at the tip and pipe bears' features as desired.

Chirpy Chick Buns
ひよこパン

Makes 6 buns

1 portion basic bread dough using 160 g bread flour (page 22)

¹/₂ portion cookie crust dough (page 34)

A little cocoa powder

A little yellow food colouring

Castor sugar, as needed

Edible black food pen

1. Prepare cookie crust dough with a little cocoa powder (page 34).

2. Prepare basic bread dough (pages 22–25, steps 1–10).

3. Set aside for first fermentation (page 26, steps 11–12).

4. Degas dough (page 26, step 13).

5. Take 6 g dough and mix well with some yellow food colouring. Divide into 6 portions for beaks. Shape into balls and set aside.

6. Divide remaining dough into 6 equal portions. Reshape into balls for body of chicks.

7. Cover dough and let rest for 10 minutes.

8. Gently punch each portion of dough again to remove gas. Reshape into balls for body of chicks. Arrange sealed side down on a lined baking tray.

9. Place a beak on each chick. Using a small pair of scissors, make a cut in yellow dough to create beaks.

10. Set aside for final fermentation (page 28, steps 18–20).

11. Divide cookie crust dough into 3–4 portions. Roll each portion out on cling film into a circle large enough to cover half of 3–4 chicks. Trim cookie crust dough into semi-circles with jagged ends on one side for egg shell. Gently place on top of chicks. Dust with sugar.

12. Preheat oven to 160°C (top and bottom heat, no fan).

13. Place tray on lowest rack in oven and bake for 18–20 minutes. During final 8–10 minutes of baking, cover buns with a sheet of aluminium foil or baking paper to prevent uneven or over browning.

14. Remove and place on a wire rack to cool.

15. Draw features of chicks using black edible food pen. Draw feet for chicks without cookie crust egg shell.

Springtime Sakura Buns

さくらパン

Makes 6 buns

1 portion basic bread dough using 160 g bread flour (page 22)

10 g sakura paste or a little pink food colouring

60 g adzuki bean paste, divided into 6 portions

6 pickled sakura flowers, rinsed and pat dry

1. Prepare basic bread dough (pages 22–25, steps 1–10).

2. Colour dough pink using sakura paste or pink food colouring.

3. Set aside for first fermentation (page 26, steps 11–12).

4. Degas dough and divide into 6 equal portions. Reshape into balls, cover and let rest for 10 minutes (pages 26–27, steps 13–15).

5. Flatten dough, then stuff with bean paste and reshape into balls (pages 30–31). Place sealed side down on a lined baking tray.

6. Using your palm, flatten buns slightly, then use a scrapper to make 5 cuts around each bun to create a 5-petal flower.

7. Using your thumb, make an indentation in the centre of buns, then press a pickled sakura flower into each indentation.

8. Set aside for final fermentation (page 28, steps 18–20).

9. Preheat oven to 150°C (top and bottom heat, no fan).

10. Place tray on lowest rack in oven and bake for 20–22 minutes. During final 8–10 minutes of baking, cover buns with a sheet of aluminium foil or baking paper to prevent uneven or over browning.

11. Remove and place on a wire rack to cool.

Cosy Koala Buns
コアラパン

Makes 6 buns

6 whole almonds

1 portion basic bread dough using 160 g bread flour (page 22)

1 portion black sesame filling (page 33), divided into 6 portions

10 g adzuki bean paste or 12 chocolate chips

Egg Wash

1 egg yolk

2 tsp milk

A pinch of salt

1. Prepare basic bread dough (pages 22–25, steps 1–10).

2. Set aside for first fermentation (page 26, steps 11–12).

3. Degas dough and divide into 6 equal portions. Reshape into balls, cover and let rest for 10 minutes (pages 26–27, steps 13–15).

4. Gently punch each portion of dough again to remove gas and divide each portion to get 2 ears (3 g each) and a head.

5. Flatten dough for heads, then stuff with black sesame filling (pages 30–31). Reshape into ovals and arrange sealed side down on a lined baking tray.

6. Shape ears into ovals and arrange on the side of heads. Using a small pair of scissors, make small cuts at the edges of ears.

7. Using a finger, make indentations in dough at positions for nose and eyes. Press an almond into dough for the nose.

8. Divide bean paste into 12 portions and shape each portion round for the eyes. Alternatively, use chocolate chips. Press into position for eyes.

9. Set aside for final fermentation (page 28, steps 18–20).

10. Combine ingredients for egg wash and brush evenly on dough.

11. Preheat oven to 170°C (top and bottom heat, no fan).

12. Place tray on lowest or second lowest rack in the oven and bake for 18–20 minutes.

13. Remove and place on a wire rack to cool.

Grab-a-Crab Buns

カニのパン

Makes 6 buns

1 portion basic bread dough using 160 g bread flour (page 22)

A little orange food colouring or 5 g dehydrated carrot powder, mixed with a little milk/water into a paste

1 portion curry chicken filling (page 32), divided into 6 portions

6 g adzuki bean paste

Red and black edible food pens

1. Prepare basic bread dough (pages 22–25, steps 1–10).

2. Colour dough orange using food colouring or carrot powder paste (page 24).

3. Set aside for first fermentation (page 26, steps 11–12).

4. Degas dough and divide into 6 equal portions. Reshape into balls, cover and let rest for 10 minutes (pages 26–27, steps 13–15).

5. Gently punch each portion of dough again to remove gas and further divide each portion to get 2 pincers (4 g each), 2 sets of legs (2 g each) and the body.

6. Flatten dough for bodies, then stuff with curry chicken filling and reshape into ovals (pages 30–31). Arrange sealed side down on a lined baking tray.

7. Shape pincers into teardrop shapes and arrange at the side of crab bodies, pointed side out. Using a small pair of scissors, make a cut at the pointed end of each pincer.

8. Shape legs into a rectangular piece and make 3 cuts on one long side using a scraper. Arrange on the side of crab bodies.

9. Using a straw, make indentations on dough at the position for eyes.

10. Divide bean paste into 12 portions and shape each portion round for the eyes. Press into position on dough.

11. Set aside for final fermentation (page 28, steps 18–20).

12. Preheat oven to 150°C (top and bottom heat, no fan).

13. Place tray on lowest rack in oven and bake for 18–20 minutes. During final 8–10 minutes of baking, cover buns with a sheet of aluminium foil or baking paper to prevent uneven or over browning.

14. Remove and place on a wire rack to cool.

15. Draw a mouth and a cross on each crab using black and red edible food pens.

Witty Fox Melon Pan
キツネのパン

Makes 6 buns

1 portion basic bread dough using 160 g bread flour (page 22)

1 portion black sesame filling (page 33)

A little orange food colouring or 5 g dehydrated carrot powder, mixed with a little milk/water into a paste

18 g adzuki bean paste, divided into 6 portions

$^1/_2$ portion cookie crust dough (page 34)

Castor sugar, as needed

Black edible food pen

1. Prepare basic bread dough (pages 22–25, steps 1–10).

2. Colour dough orange using food colouring or carrot powder paste (page 24).

3. Set aside for first fermentation (page 26, steps 11–12).

4. Degas dough and divide into 6 equal portions. Reshape into balls, cover and let rest for 10 minutes (pages 26–27, steps 13–15).

5. Gently punch each portion of dough again to remove gas and further divide each portion to get 2 ears (3 g each) and the head.

6. Flatten dough for heads, then stuff with black sesame filling and reshape into ovals (pages 30–31). Arrange sealed side down on a lined baking tray.

7. Shape ears into triangles and arrange on the side of heads on baking tray.

8. Shape bean paste into triangles and place on heads for noses.

9. Set aside for final fermentation (page 28, steps 18–20).

10. Divide cookie crust dough into 6 portions. Roll each portion out on cling film into a circle large enough to cover lower half of heads. Using a large heart-shape cutter, cut cookie crust dough and gently place on heads to resemble muzzles.

11. Cut leftover cookie crust dough into triangles and place on ears.

12. Dust cookie crust dough with sugar.

13. Preheat oven to 150°C (top and bottom heat, no fan).

14. Place tray on lowest rack in oven and bake for 18–20 minutes.

15. Remove and place on a wire rack to cool.

16. Draw eyes of foxes using black edible food pen.

King of the Jungle Buns
ライオンパン

Makes 6 buns

1 portion basic bread dough using 160 g bread flour (page 22)

A little cocoa powder, mixed with a little milk/water into a paste

Chocolate chips or chopped chocolate, as needed

Black edible food pen

Egg Wash

1 egg yolk

2 tsp milk

A pinch of salt

1. Prepare basic bread dough (pages 22–25, steps 1–10).

2. Take 100 g dough and colour it brown using cocoa powder paste (page 24). Reshape into a ball.

3. Set aside for first fermentation (page 26, steps 11–12).

4. Degas dough and divide both plain and brown dough into 6 equal portions each. Reshape into balls, cover and let rest for 10 minutes (pages 26–27, steps 13–15).

5. Gently punch each portion of dough again to remove gas.

6. Divide each ball of plain dough to get 2 ears (2 g each) and the head.

7. Flatten dough for heads, then stuff with chocolate and reshape into balls (pages 30–31).

8. Shape each portion of brown dough into a cylindrical shape long enough to wrap around each head for the lion's mane. Wrap brown dough around heads and pinch ends to seal. Place on a lined baking tray.

9. Shape ears into balls and arrange beside heads.

10. Using a small pair of scissors, make cuts all around brown dough for lion's mane.

11. Set aside for final fermentation (page 28, steps 18–20).

12. Combine ingredients for egg wash and brush evenly on plain dough.

13. Preheat oven to 170°C (top and bottom heat, no fan).

14. Place tray on lowest or second lowest rack in oven and bake for 16–18 minutes.

15. Remove and place on a wire rack to cool.

16. Draw features of lions using black edible food pen.

Sausage Dog Buns
犬のソーセージパン

Makes 6 buns

1 portion basic bread dough using 160 g bread flour (page 22)

A little cocoa powder, mixed with a little milk/water into a paste

30 g adzuki bean paste

Brown edible food pen

1 slice ham, cut into 6 ovals

6 sausages, scored and grilled

Egg Wash

1 egg yolk

2 tsp milk

A pinch of salt

1. Prepare basic bread dough (pages 22–25, steps 1–10).

2. Take 24 g dough and colour it brown using cocoa powder paste (page 24). Reshape into a ball.

3. Set aside for first fermentation (page 26, steps 11–12).

4. Degas dough and divide plain dough into 6 equal portions and brown dough into 12 equal portions. Reshape into balls, cover and let rest for 10 minutes (pages 26–27, steps 13–15).

5. Gently punch each portion of dough again to remove gas.

6. Shape plain dough into balls for heads and place sealed side down on a lined baking tray.

7. Shape brown dough into ovals for ears and arrange on side of heads.

8. Divide bean paste into 6 equal portions, then further divide each portion into 4 parts. Shape 2 parts into ovals for eyes. Combine remaining 2 parts and shape into a larger oval for the nose.

9. Press eyes and noses into position on heads.

10. Set aside for final fermentation (page 28, steps 18–20).

11. Combine ingredients for egg wash and brush evenly on dough.

12. Preheat oven to 160°C (top and bottom heat, no fan).

13. Place tray on lowest or second lowest rack in oven and bake for 18–20 minutes.

14. Remove and place on a wire rack to cool.

15. Slice buns to create mouths. Place a piece of ham into each bun to resemble a tongue. Place a grilled sausage into each bun.

Makes 8 buns

8 cashew nut halves

1 portion basic bread dough using 200 g bread flour (page 22)

A little bamboo charcoal powder, mixed with a little milk/water into a paste

Melted chocolate, as needed

4 pink heart-shaped sprinkles, cut in half

Black and pink edible food pens

Chocolate-coated biscuit sticks

1. Prepare basic bread dough (pages 22–25, steps 1–10).

2. Take 8 g dough and colour it black using bamboo charcoal powder paste (page 24). Reshape into a ball.

3. Set aside for first fermentation (page 26, steps 11–12).

4. Degas dough and divide plain dough into 8 equal portions. Reshape into balls, cover and let rest for 10 minutes (pages 26–27, steps 13–15).

5. Gently punch each portion of dough again to remove gas. Cut about one-quarter of dough from each portion of plain dough and flatten with a rolling pin. Use an animal head-shaped cookie cutter to cut shapes for heads. Reserve excess dough for tails.

6. Shape remaining portions of plain dough into balls for bodies.

7. Pinch bits of black dough and press randomly into 4 bodies to create patches for cows. Reshape into balls and arrange on a lined baking tray. Reserve any excess black dough for tails.

8. Position heads on bodies.

9. Use excess plain and black dough to make tails and place on the back of bodies.

10. Set aside for final fermentation (page 28, steps 18–20).

11. Preheat oven to 140°C (top and bottom heat, no fan).

12. Place tray on lowest rack in oven and bake for 20–22 minutes. During final 10–12 minutes of baking, cover buns with a sheet of aluminium foil or baking paper to prevent uneven or over browning.

13. Remove and place on a wire rack to cool.

14. Use melted chocolate to stick heart-shaped sprinkles on cow heads and cashew nut halves on sheep heads for horns.

15. Use black and pink edible food pens to draw features on cows and sheep.

16. Cut chocolate-coated biscuit sticks into short lengths for legs. Use a skewer to make holes at the appropriate positions under cow and sheep bodies, then insert a biscuit stick into each hole.

All Things Delicious

Sweet & Savoury Buns

Ebi Fry Buns
エビフライパン

Makes 6 buns

1 portion basic bread dough using 160 g bread flour (page 22)

A little red food colouring

12 g curry powder, mixed with a little water into a paste

6 small slices of cheese

6 sausages

A dash of ground white pepper

A pinch of salt

Olive oil, as needed

Panko, as needed

Egg Wash

1 egg yolk

2 tsp milk

A pinch of salt

1. Prepare basic bread dough (pages 22–25, steps 1–10).

2. Take 15 g dough and colour it red using red food colouring. Reshape into a ball.

3. Colour remaining dough yellow using curry powder paste (page 24). Reshape into a ball.

4. Set aside for first fermentation (page 26, steps 11–12).

5. Degas dough and divide both red and yellow dough into 6 equal portions each. Reshape into balls, cover and let rest for 10 minutes (pages 26–27, steps 13–15).

6. Gently punch each portion of dough again to remove gas.

7. Shape red dough into V-shapes and taper ends for tail of *ebi* (prawn).

8. Gently flatten each portion of yellow dough into an oval and place a slice of cheese and a sausage on top. Season with pepper and salt and pinch edges of dough to seal. Place sealed side down on a lined baking tray.

9. Place tail at one end to complete *ebi*.

10. Set aside for final fermentation (page 28, steps 18–20).

11. Combine ingredients for egg wash and brush evenly on yellow dough. Sprinkle with panko and drizzle lightly with olive oil.

12. Preheat oven to 180°C (top and bottom heat, no fan).

13. Place tray on second lowest rack in oven and bake for 18–20 minutes.

14. Remove and place on a wire rack to cool.

Golden Brown Taiyaki Buns
たい焼きパン

Makes 6 buns

1 portion basic bread dough
using 160 g bread flour
(page 22)

6 g adzuki bean paste
or 6 chocolate chips

Filling

60 g adzuki bean paste,
divided into 6 portions

1 portion custard cream
(page 33)

Egg Wash

1 egg yolk

2 tsp milk

A pinch of salt

1. Prepare basic bread dough
   (pages 22–25, steps 1–10).

2. Set aside for first fermentation
   (page 26, steps 11–12).

3. Degas dough and divide into
   6 equal portions. Reshape into balls,
   cover and let rest for 10 minutes
   (pages 26–27, steps 13–15).

4. Gently punch each portion of dough
   again to remove gas.

5. Shape into ovals and flatten. Stuff
   with a portion of bean paste or
   1 Tbsp custard cream. Fold dough
   in half to create a long semi-circular
   shape for body of fish and pinch
   edges to seal.

6. Use a scraper to make 2 diagonal
   cuts at one end of fish for tail.
   Be careful not to cut through and
   expose the filling. Place on a lined
   baking tray.

7. Using a small round cutter, make an
   indentation for eye.

8. Divide 6 g bean paste into 6 portions
   and shape into balls. Press into
   indentation for eye. Alternatively,
   use chocolate chips.

9. Use a small pair of scissors to make
   cuts on body of fish for the scales.

10. Set aside for final fermentation
    (page 28, steps 18–20).

11. Combine ingredients for egg wash
    and brush evenly on dough.

12. Preheat oven to 170°C (top and
    bottom heat, no fan).

13. Place tray on lowest rack in oven
    and bake for 16–18 minutes.

14. Remove and place on a wire rack
    to cool.

Pick-a-Mushroom Buns
キノコのパン

Makes 5 buns

1 portion basic bread dough using 200 g bread flour (page 22)

3.5 g cocoa powder, mixed with a little milk/water into a paste

50 g adzuki bean paste, divided into 5 portions

Bread flour or snow powder

1. Prepare basic bread dough (pages 22–25, steps 1–10).

2. Take 270 g dough and colour it brown using cocoa powder paste (page 24). Reshape into a ball.

3. Set aside for first fermentation (page 26, steps 11–12).

4. Degas dough and divide both plain and brown dough into 5 equal portions each. Reshape into balls, cover and let rest for 10 minutes (pages 26–27, steps 13–15).

5. Gently punch each portion of dough again to remove gas.

6. Flatten plain dough and stuff with bean paste (pages 30–31). Place each portion into a 3-cm diameter ring cutter for mushroom stems.

7. Gently roll out each portion of brown dough into a 6–7-cm disc for mushroom caps.

8. Set aside for final fermentation (page 28, steps 18–20).

9. Use a home-made stencil or a potato masher with round holes to dust mushroom caps with bread flour. Alternatively, leave plain and decorate with snow powder after baking.

10. Place mushroom caps on ring cutters and arrange on a baking tray.

11. Preheat oven to 150°C (top and bottom heat, no fan).

12. Place tray on lowest or second lowest rack in oven and bake for 20–22 minutes.

13. Remove and place on a wire rack to cool.

14. Remove ring cutters before serving.

Pumpkin Patch Buns
かぼちゃパン

Makes 6 buns

1 portion basic bread dough using 160 g bread flour (page 22)

8 g dehydrated pumpkin powder, mixed with a little milk/water into a paste

Orange food colouring, optional

Kitchen twine, as needed

Vegetable oil, as needed

Matcha-coated biscuit sticks

1. Prepare basic bread dough (pages 22–25, steps 1–10).

2. Colour dough orange using pumpkin powder paste (page 24). Adjust colour with a little orange food colouring if a stronger colour is preferred.

3. Set aside for first fermentation (page 26, steps 11–12).

4. Degas dough and divide into 6 equal portions. Reshape into balls, cover and let rest for 10 minutes (pages 26–27, steps 13–15).

5. Gently punch each portion of dough again to remove gas.

6. Soak kitchen twine in vegetable oil, then tie it around each ball of dough 4 times to create ribs in pumpkins. Secure with a knot. Place on a lined baking tray, knot-side down.

7. Set aside for final fermentation (page 28, steps 18–20).

8. Preheat oven to 150°C (top and bottom heat, no fan).

9. Place tray on lowest rack in oven and bake for 20–22 minutes. During final 10–12 minutes of baking, cover buns with a sheet of aluminium foil or baking paper to prevent uneven or over browning.

10. Remove and place on a wire rack to cool. Cut and discard kitchen twine.

11. Cut biscuit sticks into short lengths and insert into top of pumpkins for stems.

Savoury Takoyaki Bread
たこ焼きパン

Makes 18 small buns

1 portion basic bread dough using 160 g bread flour (page 22)

10 g curry powder, mixed with a little water into a paste

9 mini sausages, each cut into 3

Takoyaki sauce, to taste

Japanese mayonnaise, to taste

Bonito flakes, to taste

Aosa seaweed flakes, to taste

Egg Wash

1 egg yolk

2 tsp milk

A pinch of salt

1. Prepare basic bread dough (pages 22–25, steps 1–10).

2. Colour dough yellow using curry powder paste (page 24). Reshape into a ball.

3. Set aside for first fermentation (page 26, steps 11–12).

4. Degas dough and divide into 18 equal portions. Reshape into balls, cover and let rest for 10 minutes (pages 26–27, steps 13–15).

5. Gently punch each portion of dough again to remove gas.

6. Flatten each portion of dough and place a slice of sausage on top. Pinch edges of dough to seal (pages 30–31). Place sealed side down on a lined baking tray. At this point, you can place 6 balls together in 2 rolls of 3, like how *takoyaki* is usually served, or individually.

7. Set aside for final fermentation (page 28, steps 18–20).

8. Combine ingredients for egg wash and brush evenly on dough.

9. Preheat oven to 180°C (top and bottom heat, no fan).

10. Place tray on second lowest rack in oven and bake for 16–18 minutes.

11. Remove and place on a wire rack to cool.

12. Just before serving, place buns in serving bowls and drizzle with *takoyaki* sauce and mayonnaise. Sprinkle with bonito flakes and *aosa* seaweed flakes and serve immediately.

Pineapple Melon Pan
パイナップルのメロンパン

Makes 6 buns

1 portion cookie crust dough
(page 34)

A little yellow food colouring

1 portion basic bread dough
using 160 g bread flour
(page 22)

1.5 g matcha powder, mixed
with a little milk/water into
a paste

120 g pineapple tart filling,
divided into 6 portions

Castor sugar, as needed

1. Prepare cookie crust dough with a
   little yellow food colouring (page 34).

2. Prepare basic bread dough
   (pages 22–25, steps 1–10).

3. Take 60 g dough and colour it
   green using matcha powder paste
   (page 24).

4. Set aside for first fermentation
   (page 26, steps 11–12).

5. Degas dough and divide both plain
   and green dough into 6 equal
   portions each. Reshape into balls,
   cover and let rest for 10 minutes
   (pages 26–27, steps 13–15).

6. Gently punch each portion of dough
   again to remove gas.

7. Flatten each portion of plain dough
   and stuff with a portion of pineapple
   tart filling. Pinch edges to seal
   (pages 30–31). Place sealed side
   down on a lined baking tray.

8. Shape each portion of green dough
   into a rectangular shape, then use
   scissors to cut out about 4 triangles
   on one long side to create pineapple
   leaves. Arrange on one end of plain
   dough to form pineapples.

9. Set aside for final fermentation
   (page 28, steps 18–20).

10. Divide cookie crust dough into 6
    equal portions. Roll each portion
    out on cling film into a circle large
    enough to cover plain dough.

11. Using cling film, gently transfer a
    cookie crust circle onto each ball of
    plain dough, shaping cookie crust
    around dough as necessary.

12. Use a scraper to make light criss
    cross cuts on cookie crust to
    complete pineapple. Dust lightly
    with sugar.

13. Preheat oven to 150°C (top and
    bottom heat, with fan).

14. Place tray on lowest rack in oven
    and bake for 18–20 minutes.

15. Remove and place on a wire rack
    to cool.

Purple Plum Buns
プラムパン

Makes 8 buns

8 whole almonds

1 portion basic bread dough using 160 g bread flour (page 22)

5 g dehydrated purple sweet potato powder, mixed with a little milk/water into a paste

120 g dark chocolate, chopped

Matcha-coated biscuit sticks

Melted chocolate, as needed

1. Place almonds on a lined baking tray and bake at 180°C for 6–8 minutes. Set aside to cool.

2. Butter 8 small fluted brioche moulds, each about 4.5 cm in diameter.

3. Prepare basic bread dough (pages 22–25, steps 1–10).

4. Colour dough purple using sweet potato powder paste (page 24).

5. Set aside for first fermentation (page 26, steps 11–12).

6. Degas dough and divide into 8 equal portions. Reshape into balls, cover and let rest for 10 minutes (pages 26–27, steps 13–15).

7. Gently punch each portion of dough again to remove gas.

8. Flatten each portion of dough and stuff with some dark chocolate. Pinch edges to seal (pages 30–31). Place sealed side down in prepared brioche moulds.

9. Set aside for final fermentation (page 28, steps 18–20).

10. Preheat oven to 140°C (top and bottom heat, no fan).

11. Place tray on lowest rack in oven and bake for 20–22 minutes. During final 10–12 minutes of baking, cover buns with a sheet of aluminium foil or baking paper to prevent uneven or over browning.

12. Remove and place on a wire rack to cool.

13. Cut biscuit sticks into short lengths and insert into top of plums for stems. Use melted chocolate to stick an almond beside stems for leaves.

I Heart You Buns
ハートのパン

Makes 6 buns

1 portion basic bread dough using 160 g bread flour (page 22)

5 g dehydrated cranberry powder, mixed with a little milk/water into a paste

1. Prepare basic bread dough (pages 22–25, steps 1–10).

2. Colour dough pink using cranberry powder paste (page 24). Reshape into a ball.

3. Set aside for first fermentation (page 26, steps 11–12).

4. Degas dough and divide into 6 equal portions. Reshape into balls, cover and let rest for 10 minutes (pages 26–27, steps 13–15).

5. Gently punch dough again to remove gas.

6. Shape each portion of dough into an oblong and taper the ends.

7. Bring the ends together and use a scraper to make a cut at the wider end. Open up the cut to create a heart shape. Arrange on a lined baking tray.

8. Set aside for final fermentation (page 28, steps 18–20).

9. Preheat oven to 140°C (top and bottom heat, no fan).

10. Place tray on lowest rack in oven and bake for 20–22 minutes. During final 10–12 minutes of baking, cover buns with a sheet of aluminium foil or baking paper to prevent uneven or over browning.

11. Remove and place on a wire rack to cool.

12. Slice buns across in half and fill with your favourite sandwich filling.

Tear Me Up

Pull-Apart Bread

Three Little Pigs-on-a-Stick Bread
ブタさんのだんごパン

Makes 18 small buns

1 portion basic bread dough
   using 160 g bread flour
   (page 22)

Black edible food pen

1 slice ham

1. Prepare basic bread dough
   (pages 22–25, steps 1–10).

2. Set aside for first fermentation
   (page 26, steps 11–12).

3. Degas dough and divide into
   6 equal portions. Reshape into balls,
   cover and let rest for 10 minutes
   (pages 26–27, steps 13–15).

4. Gently punch dough again to remove
   gas, then further divide each portion
   into 3.

5. Shape into balls and arrange in rows
   of 3, sealed side down, on a lined
   baking tray.

6. Use a small pair of scissors to make
   2 cuts at the tip of each ball for ears.

7. Use a small ring cutter to cut 18
   rounds from ham, then use a small
   straw to cut 2 holes from ham
   to create snouts. Press ham into
   position on dough.

8. Set aside for final fermentation
   (page 28, steps 18–20).

9. Preheat oven to 140°C (top and
   bottom heat, no fan).

10. Place tray on lowest or second
    lowest rack in oven and bake for
    20–22 minutes. During final
    8–10 minutes of baking, cover
    buns with a sheet of aluminium foil
    or baking paper to prevent uneven
    or over browning.

11. Remove and place on a wire rack
    to cool.

12. Draw features using black edible
    food pen, then insert a skewer
    through each row of pigs.

Panda Friends-on-a-Stick Bread
パンダさんのだんごパン

Makes 18 small buns

1 portion basic bread dough using 160 g bread flour (page 22)

A little bamboo charcoal powder, mixed with a little milk/water into a paste

Black and pink edible food pens

1. Prepare basic bread dough (pages 22–25, steps 1–10).

2. Take 36 g dough and colour it black using bamboo charcoal powder paste (page 24).

3. Set aside for first fermentation (page 26, steps 11–12).

4. Degas dough. Divide plain dough into 6 equal portions and reshape into balls. Cover both plain and black dough and let rest for 10 minutes (pages 26–27, steps 13–15).

5. Gently punch dough again to remove gas, then further divide each portion of plain dough into 3.

6. Shape plain dough into balls for panda heads and arrange in rows of 3, sealed side down, on a lined baking tray.

7. Divide black dough into 36 portions for ears. Roll each portion into a ball and arrange 2 at the top of each panda head.

8. Set aside for final fermentation (page 28, steps 18–20).

9. Preheat oven to 140°C (top and bottom heat, no fan).

10. Place tray on lowest rack in oven and bake for 20–22 minutes. During final 10–12 minutes of baking, cover buns with a sheet of aluminium foil or baking paper to prevent uneven or over browning.

11. Remove and place on a wire rack to cool.

12. Draw features using black and pink edible food pens, then insert a skewer through each row of pandas.

Two-Colour Chicks Pull-Apart Bread

チキンのちぎりパン

Makes 9 buns

1 portion basic bread dough using 200 g bread flour (page 22)

A little orange and red food colouring

8 g dehydrated pumpkin powder, mixed with a little milk/water into a paste

Black chocolate pen

1. Prepare basic bread dough (pages 22–25, steps 1–10).

2. Take 6 g dough and colour it orange and 10 g dough and colour it red using food colouring. Take 156 g dough and colour it yellow using pumpkin powder paste (page 24). Reshape into balls.

3. Set aside for first fermentation (page 26, steps 11–12).

4. Degas dough and divide plain dough into 5 equal portions and yellow dough into 4 equal portions. Reshape into balls, cover and let rest for 10 minutes (pages 26–27, steps 13–15).

5. Gently punch each portion of dough again to remove gas.

6. Reshape into balls for heads of chicks and arrange plain and yellow dough alternately in 3 rows of 3 on a lined baking tray. Leave a 1-cm gap between each ball of dough.

7. Shape orange and red dough into beaks and crowns of chicks and arrange on plain and yellow dough. Use a toothpick to press dough down and keep them in position.

8. Set aside for final fermentation (page 28, steps 18–20).

9. Preheat oven to 140°C (top and bottom heat, no fan).

10. Place tray on lowest rack in oven and bake for 20–22 minutes. During final 10–12 minutes of baking, cover buns with a sheet of aluminium foil or baking paper to prevent uneven or over browning.

11. Remove and place on a wire rack to cool.

12. Draw features of chicks using chocolate pens.

Circle of Bears Pull-Apart Bread
クマのチギリパン

Makes 6 buns

1 portion basic bread dough using 200 g bread flour (page 22)

1 portion royal icing (page 21)

Black chocolate pen

12 red heart-shaped sprinkles

Melted chocolate, as needed

1. Prepare basic bread dough (pages 22–25, steps 1–10).

2. Set aside for first fermentation (page 26, steps 11–12).

3. Degas dough and divide into 6 equal portions. Reshape into balls, cover and let rest for 10 minutes (pages 26–27, steps 13–15).

4. Gently punch each portion of dough again to remove gas.

5. Reshape into balls and further divide each portion of dough to get a body (35 g), a head (14 g), a ear (2.5 g), an arm (2.5 g) and a leg (3 g). One ear, one arm and one leg will suffice as the bears share ears and limbs.

6. Reshape into balls. Place bodies around a chiffon cake funnel, keeping them about 1 cm apart. Arrange heads, ears and limbs in place.

7. Set aside for final fermentation (page 28, steps 18–20).

8. Preheat oven to 140°C (top and bottom heat, no fan).

9. Place tray on lowest rack in oven and bake for 20–22 minutes. During final 10–12 minutes of baking, cover buns with a sheet of aluminium foil or baking paper to prevent uneven or over browning.

10. Remove and place on a wire rack to cool.

11. Draw features of bears using royal icing and black chocolate pen. Attach sprinkles for ribbons using melted chocolate.

Panda Pull-Apart Ring Bread

パンダのちぎりパン

Makes 6 buns

1 portion basic bread dough using 200 g bread flour (page 22)

A little bamboo charcoal powder, mixed with a little milk/water into a paste

Black edible food pen

1. Prepare basic bread dough (pages 22–25, steps 1–10).

2. Take 66 g dough and colour it black using bamboo charcoal powder paste (page 24).

3. Set aside for first fermentation (page 26, steps 11–12).

4. Degas dough. Divide plain dough to get 6 bodies (35 g each), then divide remaining dough equally to get 6 heads. Reshape into balls, cover and let rest for 10 minutes (pages 26–27, steps 13–15).

5. Gently punch each portion of dough again to remove gas.

6. Reshape into balls. Place bodies around a chiffon cake funnel, keeping them about 1 cm apart. Arrange heads in place.

7. Divide black dough into 3 portions, 36 g for legs, 12 g for arms and 18 g for ears. Further divide each portion into 12 equal parts to get 12 legs, 12 arms and 12 ears.

8. Shape legs and arms into ovals and ears into balls. Arrange in place.

9. Set aside for final fermentation (page 28, steps 18–20).

10. Preheat oven to 140°C (top and bottom heat, no fan).

11. Place tray on lowest rack in oven and bake for 20–22 minutes. During final 10–12 minutes of baking, cover buns with a sheet of aluminium foil or baking paper to prevent uneven or over browning.

12. Remove and place on a wire rack to cool.

13. Draw features of pandas using black edible food pen.

Snow White Pull-Apart Bread
白雪姫のちぎりパン

Makes 7 buns

1 portion basic bread dough using 200 g bread flour (page 22)

Red, pink, violet, green, blue, turquoise and yellow food colouring or other colours as desired

A little bamboo charcoal powder, mixed with a little milk/water into a paste

1/2 portion cookie crust dough (page 34)

Castor sugar, as needed

Black edible food pen

1. Prepare basic bread dough (pages 22–25, steps 1–10).

2. Take 12 g dough and colour it red. Take 6 balls of dough 10 g each and colour each portion a different colour — pink, violet, green, blue, turquoise and yellow. Take 28 g dough and colour it black using bamboo charcoal powder paste (page 24). Reshape into balls.

3. Set aside for first fermentation (page 26, steps 11–12).

4. Degas dough. Divide red dough into a 10 g portion for dwarf's hat and a 2 g portion for Snow White's hair band. Portion out 7 g plain dough and divide it into 7 parts for dwarfs' noses. Divide remaining plain dough into 8 equal portions for heads. Divide black dough into a 20 g portion and two 4 g portions for Snow White's hair. Reshape into balls, cover and let rest for 10 minutes (pages 26–27, steps 13–15).

5. Gently punch each portion of dough again to remove gas. Reshape plain dough for heads into balls.

6. Shape dwarfs' hats. Flatten red dough (10 g) into a triangle and wrap it around a head. Pinch edges to seal. Repeat with pink, violet, green, blue, turquoise and yellow dough.

7. Arrange dwarfs' heads around a chiffon cake funnel, keeping them about 1 cm apart. Place noses on dwarfs.

8. Shape Snow White's hair. Flatten black dough (20 g) into a rectangle and arrange it on the top of her head. Shape remaining black dough (4 g) into balls and place at the side of her head. Shape remaining red dough (2 g) into a strip and place it on her hair. Place on a lined baking tray.

9. Set aside for final fermentation (page 28, steps 18–20).

10. Divide cookie crust dough into 7 equal portions. Roll each portion out on cling film into a semi-circle large enough to cover bottom half of dwarfs' faces. Using cling film, gently transfer cookie crust onto each dwarf, shaping it around dough as necessary. Sprinkle with sugar.

11. Preheat oven to 140°C (top and bottom heat, no fan).

12. Place tray on lowest rack in oven and bake for 20–22 minutes. During final 10–12 minutes of baking, cover buns with a sheet of aluminium foil or baking paper to prevent uneven or over browning.

13. Remove and place on a wire rack to cool. Draw features using black edible food pen.

Kittens-in-a-Pan Pull-Apart Bread
にゃんにゃんのちぎりパン

Makes 12 buns

1 portion basic bread dough using 160 g bread flour (page 22)

3 g cocoa powder, mixed with a little milk/water into a paste

Melted chocolate, as needed

Black chocolate pen

1. Prepare basic bread dough (pages 22–25, steps 1–10).

2. Divide dough into 2 equal portions and colour one portion brown using cocoa powder paste (page 24).

3. Set aside for first fermentation (page 26, steps 11–12).

4. Degas dough and divide both plain and brown dough into 6 equal portions. Reshape into balls, cover and let rest for 10 minutes (pages 26–27, steps 13–15).

5. Gently punch each portion of dough again to remove gas.

6. Reshape into balls and further divide each portion of dough to get 2 ears (2 g each) and a head.

7. Reshape into balls. Place 2 balls of each colour in a shallow baking pan, approximately 10 x 8-cm, keeping them about 1 cm apart.

8. Flatten dough for ears and cut into triangles using a scraper. Place on a lined baking tray.

9. Set aside for final fermentation (page 28, steps 18–20).

10. Preheat oven to 140°C (top and bottom heat, no fan).

11. Place tray on lowest rack in oven and bake for 20–22 minutes. Remove ears after 6–7 minutes. During final 10–12 minutes of baking, cover buns with a sheet of aluminium foil or baking paper to prevent uneven or over browning.

12. Remove and place on a wire rack to cool.

13. Attach ears using melted chocolate and draw features of kittens using black chocolate pen.

Halloween Pull-Apart Bread
のちぎりパン

Makes 9 buns

1 portion basic bread dough using 200 g bread flour (page 22)

1 g bamboo charcoal powder, mixed with a little milk/water into a paste

3 g matcha powder, mixed with a little milk/water into a paste

1 portion royal icing (page 21)

Black edible food pen

1. Prepare basic bread dough (pages 22–25, steps 1–10).

2. Divide dough into 3 equal portions, then cut 6 g each from 2 portions and add to the 3rd portion.

3. Colour larger portion black using bamboo charcoal powder paste and one smaller portion green using matcha powder paste (page 24). Leave other portion plain. Reshape into balls.

4. Set aside for first fermentation (page 26, steps 11–12).

5. Degas dough and divide both green and plain dough into 3 equal portions each. Cut 12 g from black dough and divide remaining black dough into 3 equal portions. Reshape into balls, cover and let rest for 10 minutes (pages 26–27, steps 13–15).

6. Gently punch each portion of dough again to remove gas. Reshape into balls.

7. Divide 12 g portion of black dough into 3 parts. Flatten each portion and cut using a scraper to create hair. Place on balls of green dough.

8. On a lined baking tray, arrange black, green and plain balls of dough alternately to form 3 rows of 3, keeping them about 1 cm apart.

9. Set aside for final fermentation (page 28, steps 18–20).

10. Preheat oven to 140°C (top and bottom heat, no fan).

11. Place tray on lowest rack in oven and bake for 20–22 minutes. During final 10–12 minutes of baking, cover buns with a sheet of aluminium foil or baking paper to prevent uneven or over browning.

12. Remove and place on a wire rack to cool.

13. Decorate buns with spider webs and/or ghosts using royal icing and draw features on green and plain buns using a black edible food pen.

Enchanted Garden Bread
可愛いガーデンパン

Makes 2 large buns

1 portion basic bread dough using 200 g bread flour (page 22)

A little yellow food colouring

A little pink food colouring

5 g matcha powder, mixed with a little milk/water into a paste

Black edible food pen

Baked pasta sticks (page 20)

1. Prepare basic bread dough (pages 22–25, steps 1–10).

2. Take 25 g dough and colour it yellow and 25 g pink using food colouring. Leave 15 g plain and colour remainder green using matcha powder paste (page 24). Reshape into balls.

3. Set aside for first fermentation (page 26, steps 11–12).

4. Degas dough. Divide green dough into 2 equal portions, and yellow and pink dough into 5 equal portions each. Reshape into balls, cover and let rest for 10 minutes (pages 26–27, steps 13–15).

5. Gently punch each portion of dough to remove gas. Reshape into balls.

6. Divide pink dough into 5 equal portions, then further divide each portion into 5. Shape into balls for flower petals.

7. Divide plain dough into 10 parts for centre of flowers and bees' wings.

8. On a lined baking tray, arrange plain and pink dough to form flowers. To form bees, place a ball of plain dough on one side of yellow dough. Use a small pair of scissors to make a cut in the centre of plain dough to form wings.

9. Divide green dough into 5 equal portions each and roll into long strips. Pinch 5 strips of green dough together at one end. To braid, cross strand 5 over strand 4, and cross strand 3 over strand 5. Cross strand 1 over strand 4, and cross strand 3 over strand 1. Repeat until you get to the end of the strands. Pinch the ends together. Repeat with other set. Place on a lined baking tray.

10. Set aside for final fermentation (page 28, steps 18–20).

11. Preheat oven to 150°C (top and bottom heat, no fan).

12. Place tray on lowest rack in oven and bake for 20–22 minutes. Remove flowers and bees after 6–7 minutes. During final 10–12 minutes of baking, cover buns with a sheet of aluminium foil or baking paper to prevent uneven or over browning.

13. Remove and place on a wire rack to cool.

14. Use a black edible food pen to draw details on bees. Use baked pasta sticks to attach flowers and bees to braided loaves.

Christmas Magic Pull-Apart Bread

雪だるまはパンを外に引きます

Makes 9 buns

1 portion basic bread dough using 200 g bread flour (page 22)

Red and yellow food colouring

5 g matcha powder, mixed with a little milk/water into a paste

Black, orange and pink edible food pen

Bamboo skewers or baked pasta sticks (page 20)

Melted chocolate, as needed

Snow powder, as needed

1. Prepare basic bread dough (pages 22–25, steps 1–10).

2. Take 20 g dough and colour it yellow and 25 g dough and colour it pink using food colouring. Leave 25 g plain and colour remainder green using matcha powder paste (page 24). Reshape into balls.

3. Set aside for first fermentation (page 26, steps 11–12).

4. Degas dough. Divide green dough into 13 equal portions. Reshape into balls, cover and let rest for 10 minutes (pages 26–27, steps 13–15).

5. Gently punch each portion of dough to remove gas. Reshape into balls.

6. On a lined baking tray, arrange green balls to form a Christmas tree. Start with a ring of 5 balls, then stack 4 balls on top, followed by 3 balls and finish with a single ball.

7. Flatten yellow dough and use a star cutter to cut star shapes.

8. Take some plain dough and shape into 2 balls to form a snowman. Use remaining yellow dough to form scarf of snowman.

9. Use some red dough to form a santa's hat and some plain dough to decorate it.

10. Use remaining red and plain dough to form balls to decorate tree.

11. Place decorations on a lined baking tray.

12. Set aside for final fermentation (page 28, steps 18–20).

13. Preheat oven to 140°C (top and bottom heat, no fan).

14. Place tray on lowest rack in oven and bake for 20–22 minutes. Remove stars, snowman, santa's hat and balls after 7–8 minutes. During final 10–12 minutes of baking, cover buns with a sheet of aluminium foil or baking paper to prevent uneven or over browning.

15. Remove and place on a wire rack to cool.

16. Use edible food pens to draw details on snowman. Use bamboo skewers or baked pasta sticks and/or melted chocolate to attach decorations to tree. Dust with snow powder.

Weights & Measures

Quantities for this book are given in Metric and American (spoon) measures. Standard spoon and cup measurements used are: 1 tsp = 5 ml, 1 Tbsp = 15 ml, 1 cup = 250 ml. All measures are level unless otherwise stated.

LIQUID AND VOLUME MEASURES

Metric	Imperial	American
5 ml	$^1/_6$ fl oz	1 teaspoon
10 ml	$^1/_3$ fl oz	1 dessertspoon
15 ml	$^1/_2$ fl oz	1 tablespoon
60 ml	2 fl oz	$^1/_4$ cup (4 tablespoons)
85 ml	$2^1/_2$ fl oz	$^1/_3$ cup
90 ml	3 fl oz	$^3/_8$ cup (6 tablespoons)
125 ml	4 fl oz	$^1/_2$ cup
180 ml	6 fl oz	$^3/_4$ cup
250 ml	8 fl oz	1 cup
300 ml	10 fl oz ($^1/_2$ pint)	$1^1/_4$ cups
375 ml	12 fl oz	$1^1/_2$ cups
435 ml	14 fl oz	$1^3/_4$ cups
500 ml	16 fl oz	2 cups
625 ml	20 fl oz (1 pint)	$2^1/_2$ cups
750 ml	24 fl oz ($1^1/_5$ pints)	3 cups
1 litre	32 fl oz ($1^3/_5$ pints)	4 cups
1.25 litres	40 fl oz (2 pints)	5 cups
1.5 litres	48 fl oz ($2^2/_5$ pints)	6 cups
2.5 litres	80 fl oz (4 pints)	10 cups

DRY MEASURES

Metric	Imperial
30 grams	1 ounce
45 grams	$1^1/_2$ ounces
55 grams	2 ounces
70 grams	$2^1/_2$ ounces
85 grams	3 ounces
100 grams	$3^1/_2$ ounces
110 grams	4 ounces
125 grams	$4^1/_2$ ounces
140 grams	5 ounces
280 grams	10 ounces
450 grams	16 ounces (1 pound)
500 grams	1 pound, $1^1/_2$ ounces
700 grams	$1^1/_2$ pounds
800 grams	$1^1/_2$ pounds
1 kilogram	2 pounds, 3 ounces
1.5 kilograms	3 pounds, $4^1/_2$ ounces
2 kilograms	4 pounds, 6 ounces

OVEN TEMPERATURE

	°C	°F	Gas Regulo
Very slow	120	250	1
Slow	150	300	2
Moderately slow	160	325	3
Moderate	180	350	4
Moderately hot	190/200	370/400	5/6
Hot	210/220	410/440	6/7
Very hot	230	450	8
Super hot	250/290	475/550	9/10

LENGTH

Metric	Imperial
0.5 cm	$^1/_4$ inch
1 cm	$^1/_2$ inch
1.5 cm	$^3/_4$ inch
2.5 cm	1 inch

ABBREVIATION

tsp	teaspoon
Tbsp	Tablespoon
g	gram
kg	kilogram
ml	millilitre